6

AF283933

# Hope on Turtle Island

By Paul Shipton

Illustrated by Carl Pearce

Activities by Hannah Fish

## Contents

### OXFORD
UNIVERSITY PRESS

# Meet the Characters

Ben and Rosie are always ready for a new adventure in Grandpa's amazing van.

The van can fly. It can change shape. It can go anywhere in the world in moments …

Ben and Rosie are ready for their next adventure. Are *you*?

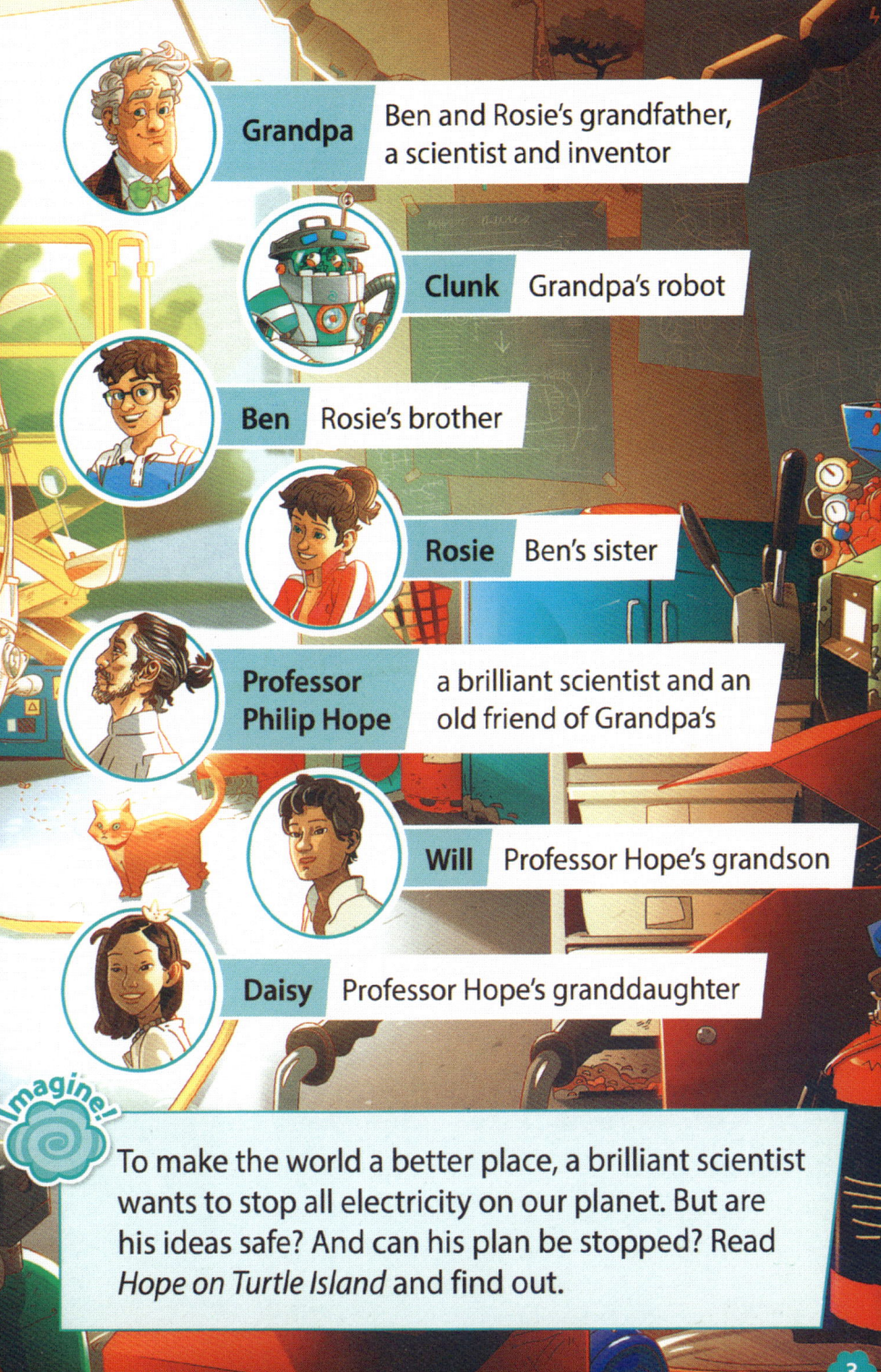

**Grandpa** Ben and Rosie's grandfather, a scientist and inventor

**Clunk** Grandpa's robot

**Ben** Rosie's brother

**Rosie** Ben's sister

**Professor Philip Hope** a brilliant scientist and an old friend of Grandpa's

**Will** Professor Hope's grandson

**Daisy** Professor Hope's granddaughter

Imagine!

To make the world a better place, a brilliant scientist wants to stop all electricity on our planet. But are his ideas safe? And can his plan be stopped? Read *Hope on Turtle Island* and find out.

# Chapter One

'Would you like a plastic bag?' asked the woman behind the counter.

'Sure,' said Rosie. 'Thank you.' She was buying a new sweater in her favorite store.

'Wait,' said Ben, who had met Rosie in town for a coffee. 'You don't need a plastic bag. I can carry your sweater in my backpack.'

Rosie smiled. 'OK Ben, I know, I know – we shouldn't use too many plastic bags! Here.' She gave her new sweater to Ben. 'Just don't let it get dirty in your backpack!'

Outside, Rosie asked, 'Do you want to go to another store?'

'No,' said Ben. 'Let's go home.'

They began to walk to the bus stop.

Ten minutes later, they were on the bus.

Rosie was listening to music on her phone, while Ben was reading a text message from a friend.

Suddenly …

'There's a problem with my phone,' said Rosie.

'There's a problem with my phone, too,' said Ben. 'The screen's gone blank.'

They looked around; the same was true for everyone on the bus. All the people on the sidewalk were also looking unhappily at their phones. All the screens in a store window were blank, too.

'What's happening?' asked Rosie.

→ Go to page 36 for activities.

Suddenly a man's voice began to speak on all the phones: 'Hello, people of the world!'

Ben looked at Rosie. 'Is this a joke?'

'We live on a wonderful planet,' said the voice. 'It gives us air to breathe, water to drink, and food to eat. But we must care for this beautiful home! Pollution is getting worse. Every year, more and more rainforests are destroyed, more animals and plants disappear ... But don't be worried! It isn't too late for us to change the way that we live!'

'I have a wonderful machine that can stop *anything* that uses electricity,' the voice said. 'Just think – no more electric lights, no more computers, nothing. Without batteries, cell phones and tablets won't work. Cars and planes will have to stop. We will be free to return to a simpler life!'

Ben and Rosie listened nervously.

'To show you, I will use my Earth Machine to stop all the power to just one city,' said the man. 'But soon I'll be ready to use it across the world!'

'Do you believe him?' Rosie asked.

As they got off the bus, Ben looked around. The bus and all the cars were stopping. All the lights were off.

'Yes,' he said.

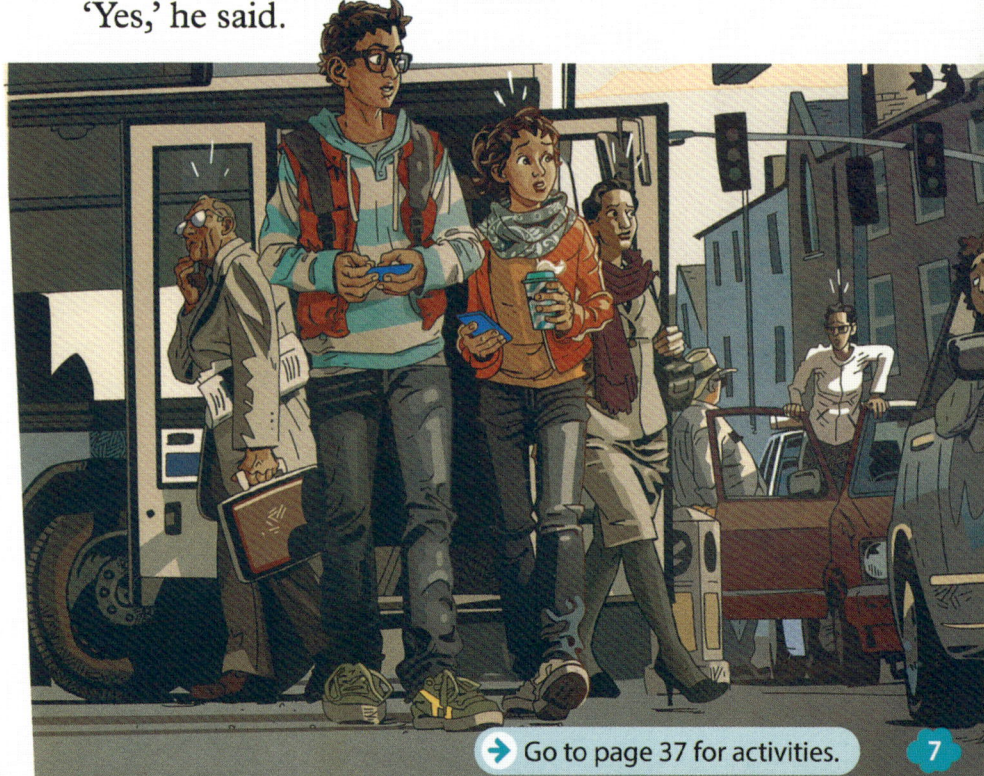

→ Go to page 37 for activities.

## Chapter Two

The streets were quiet as Ben and Rosie ran home. No cars or buses were moving. There were no lights, and no sound of music from any radio.

'Who was that man?' asked Rosie. 'Was he really speaking to everyone in the world?'

'I don't know,' said Ben. 'But he wasn't lying about his machine. He chose our city to show how it works!'

'I don't like this,' said Rosie. 'I'm scared!'

'Me, too,' said Ben. 'But Grandpa will know what to do. Grandpa always knows what to do!'

They didn't stop running until they reached the house.

Inside, they hurried to Grandpa's office and opened the door. The office was dark.

'Grandpa? Grandpa, are you in here?' Ben asked nervously.

There was no answer.

Suddenly all the lights came back on.

'That man must have turned his machine off again,' said Ben.

'What's happening?' asked a robotic voice behind them. Clunk was at the door.

'I don't know,' said Ben.

Rosie pointed at Grandpa's empty chair. 'We thought that Grandpa might know … but where is he?'

→ Go to page 38 for activities.

Clunk went to the computer. 'A few years ago, someone tried to steal some of Grandpa's work,' he said. 'So now, Grandpa always keeps the computer camera on to record everything in the room.'

Clunk hit some keys on the keyboard. Now the screen showed everything that had happened in Grandpa's office twenty minutes earlier. Ben and Rosie saw Grandpa working; then suddenly he looked up and started to listen to something from the computer.

'That must be when that strange message arrived,' said Ben.

They watched Grandpa on the screen as he quickly wrote something in his notebook.

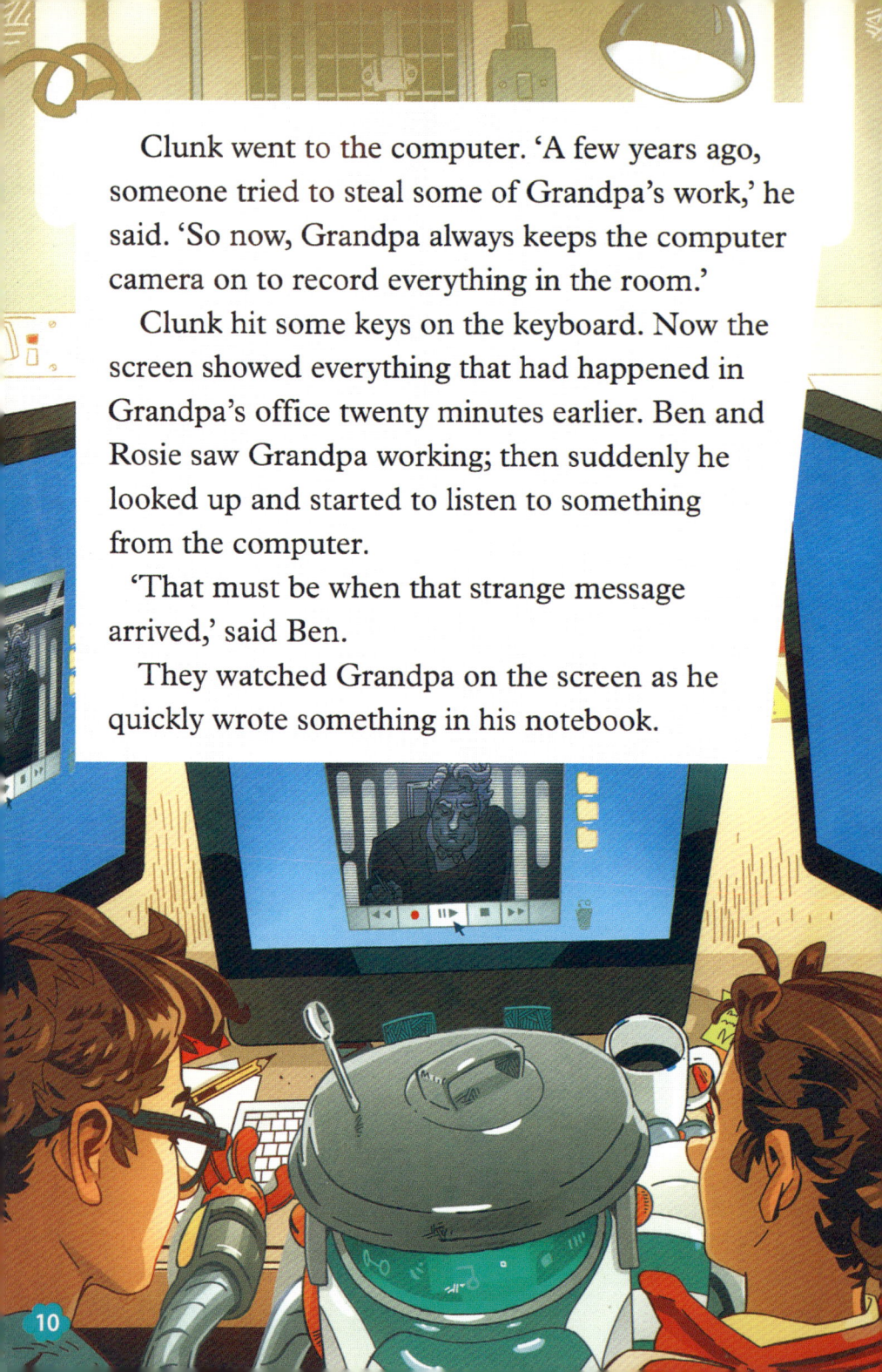

Rosie looked at the notebook now. Under a little drawing of an animal, Grandpa had written just one word: "HOPE?"

'What does *that* mean?' asked Rosie.

Ben was still watching the computer screen. 'Look!' he said. 'Grandpa called someone on his cell phone.'

On the screen, Grandpa spoke into his phone for a few seconds. Then suddenly there was a flash of light, and he disappeared.

'What happened?' asked Rosie. 'Is Grandpa OK? Where is he now?'

Clunk moved to the door. 'I know where Grandpa is,' he said.

→ Go to page 39 for activities.

## Chapter Three

Clunk was already in the van when Ben and Rosie ran outside.

'Wait, Clunk!' shouted Ben. 'Are you going to get Grandpa? We want to come, too.'

'I'm sorry,' said Clunk. 'It's too dangerous.'

Ben and Rosie stood in front of the van. 'If Grandpa's in a dangerous place, we *all* have to help him!' said Rosie.

Clunk thought about this.

'We're not going to move until you say yes,' said Ben. He and Rosie put their hands on the front of the van.

Clunk knew that he wasn't going to be able to leave without them.

'OK,' he said at last. 'Get in the van, please.'

Moments later, the van was in a very different kind of place – a beach. Ben and Rosie looked at the sand and the beautiful, blue sea.

'Is this an island?' asked Rosie.

'Yes,' said Clunk. 'It's called Turtle Island.'

'So this is where Grandpa is,' said Ben. 'But why is he here? And how are we going to find him?'

Clunk started to explain. 'Grandpa's here because –' He stopped suddenly.

'What's wrong?' asked Rosie.

The robot pointed down the beach. Two dark shapes were coming toward them.

'What are those things?' asked Ben.

→ Go to page 40 for activities.

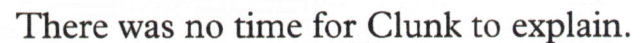

There was no time for Clunk to explain.

'Quick,' he said. 'Follow me!' He began to move up the beach toward the trees.

Rosie looked over her shoulder. Now she could see what the things on the beach were – robots!

'I thought that only Grandpa could make robots like Clunk!' said Ben.

But these tall robots were very different from Clunk. They looked fast and strong ... and *dangerous*!

Clunk had stopped – he had reached a fence.

'Can we climb over it?' asked Rosie.

'I'll try,' said Clunk.

As soon as the little robot touched the fence, there was a flash of bright light.

Clunk fell back.

'Clunk! Are you OK?' asked Rosie.

'It must be an electric fence!' said Ben.

They looked down at Clunk. He wasn't moving.

Suddenly there was a sound from behind them. The robots from the beach were here.

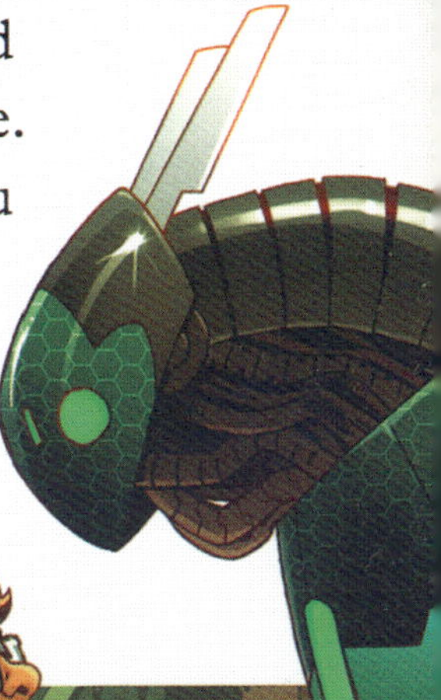

Ben turned and looked up. 'What do you want with us?' he asked.

'Follow us,' said the first robot. 'You must meet the Professor.'

'What about Clunk?' asked Rosie.

She turned and looked at the ground. But Clunk was not there …

→ Go to page 41 for activities.

# Chapter Four

Ben and Rosie followed the robots away from the beach. They didn't try to run away – they knew that the robots were much faster than they were. Also, there were too many questions that they wanted the answers to. The robots had spoken about a professor. Was he the same person who had stopped the electricity in their city? And what about Grandpa – was he here on this island? And if Grandpa *was* here, *why*?

They climbed for a few minutes until at last they saw a large building in the middle of the island.

They followed the robots until soon they were standing outside a big, metal door at the front of the building. A camera above the door moved up and down – someone was studying Ben and Rosie carefully.

They waited nervously. What were they going to find behind that metal door?

A moment later, the door began to open.

'Be brave,' said Ben quietly to his sister. 'Remember – we're here to help Grandpa.'

As the door opened, Rosie saw that someone was waiting to meet them. But who?

Go to page 42 for activities.

Two other teenagers – a boy and a girl – were waiting on the other side of the door.

'Hello!' said the boy with a smile. He was about as old as Ben.

The girl was smiling, too. 'You must be Ben and Rosie!'

Ben and Rosie were surprised. They didn't understand what was happening.

'Who are *you*?' asked Ben.

'And how do you know our names?' added Rosie.

'I'm Daisy,' said the girl. 'This is my big brother, Will.'

'We've heard a lot about you two,' said Will.

'Don't be worried,' laughed Daisy. 'You're here for your grandpa, aren't you? He's safe. Come on – we'll take you to him.'

'And then *our* grandfather can explain everything to you,' said Will.

Will and Daisy started to take Ben and Rosie to a different part of the building.

At last they came to a big room with lots of machines.

A thin man in a white coat looked up. 'Welcome,' he said. 'My name is Professor Hope.'

Ben and Rosie knew that voice – this was the man who had sent the strange message on their phones!

→ Go to page 43 for activities.

## Chapter Five

Another man was in the room, too – Grandpa! He looked worried when he saw Ben and Rosie.

'You shouldn't have come here,' he told them.

Professor Hope smiled. 'I'm happy to have them here. We don't have many visitors on Turtle Island!' Hope's smile disappeared. 'Of course, there are no turtles here now. They used to come to lay their eggs. I loved to watch the baby turtles as they ran to the sea. But with more and more pollution in the sea, the turtles stopped coming.'

'But everything will be better after you use the Earth Machine,' said Will happily.

'That's right!' said Hope. He pointed to a huge machine. 'The test on your city worked well. Soon my machine will be ready to use on every city in the world!' He checked a clock on the side of the machine – its numbers moved from 60 down to 59. '*Very* soon – in just fifty-nine minutes!'

'That's terrible!' said Rosie. 'How will people live with no electricity?'

'They'll live more simply!' said Hope. 'They can grow their own food. They won't need to travel so far. It will be a wonderful new start!'

→ Go to page 44 for activities.

'You're wrong, Philip,' Grandpa said quietly. 'We need to care for our planet, but this isn't the way to do it. Your idea is dangerous.'

Hope gave Grandpa a disappointed look. 'I thought that you would understand, my old friend. I was surprised when you called and asked me to stop my plan.'

Ben understood what had happened. 'So after Grandpa called you, you used one of your machines to bring him here?' he asked.

'Yes, of course!' said Hope. 'I couldn't let anyone try to stop me ... and I can't let you stop me now.'

Hope turned to one of his robots. 'Take our three visitors to one of the rooms downstairs,' he said. 'And don't forget to lock the door!'

'Follow me,' the robot said to Ben, Rosie, and Grandpa.

Will and Daisy looked worried as the others left the room.

Grandpa turned to Professor Hope. 'Please think again, Philip. This plan isn't going to help our planet. It's going to make more problems all around the world!'

As he left, Ben looked nervously at the clock on Hope's Earth Machine. There wasn't much time to stop Hope's plan!

→ Go to page 45 for activities.

## Chapter Six

Ben, Rosie, and Grandpa sat in an empty room.

'Where's Clunk?' asked Grandpa. 'Why wasn't he with you?'

Rosie quickly explained about the little robot. 'I hope that he's OK,' she added.

'So how do you know Professor Hope?' Ben asked Grandpa.

'We used to be best friends,' said Grandpa. 'Philip Hope was a brilliant scientist! At first he wanted only to make the world a better place. But when nobody listened to his ideas, he became angry. He forgot about everyone except his family. He moved to this island and I didn't hear from him for years.'

Ben looked nervously at his watch. 'Hope will use his machine in about forty minutes! How can we stop him?'

Suddenly there was a loud noise at the wall. Something was hitting it hard.

Rosie could guess who was making that noise. She just hoped that she was right.

A moment later, there was a big hole in the wall! A little face looked through that hole.

'Hello,' said Clunk.

'Clunk, you're OK!' shouted Rosie.

'I'm sorry that I'm late,' said Clunk. 'It wasn't easy finding you.'

There was a sound from the other side of the door. 'Hope's robots are coming!' said Ben.

→ Go to page 46 for activities.

Grandpa turned to Rosie. 'You're the fastest runner,' he said. 'Go to the van as fast as you can! We'll try and stop Hope's robots here.'

'What shall I do when I get to the van?' asked Rosie.

'Leave this island,' said Grandpa. 'You have to tell the police what's happening here. Quick!'

Rosie didn't say another word. She jumped through the hole in the wall and began to run to the trees.

Moments later, the door opened and two of Hope's robots came into the room.

Professor Hope was watching everything on a big screen.

'The girl isn't in the room!' he shouted to his robots. 'Go after her! You mustn't let her reach that van!'

Will and Daisy watched their grandfather nervously. They had never seen him this angry before.

Outside, Rosie ran as fast as she could. Soon she was tired and her legs hurt, but she didn't stop.

When she heard a sound through the trees behind her, she didn't look back. She didn't have to – she knew that Hope's robots were coming.

→ Go to page 47 for activities.

## Chapter Seven

Rosie ran.

She tried not to think about Hope's Earth Machine or the robots behind her. She tried not to think about the future of the world if she didn't reach the van.

The electric fence was in front of her now, and she saw a hole that Clunk had made in it. Rosie ran through it.

'FASTER!' she told herself.

Now she could see the van on the beach. She was getting closer and closer …

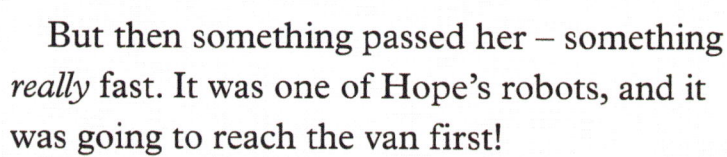

But then something passed her – something *really* fast. It was one of Hope's robots, and it was going to reach the van first!

Hope was watching everything on his screen.

'Now destroy that van!' he told the robot on the beach.

Hope's other robots had brought Grandpa, Ben, and Clunk back to the room with the Earth Machine. Will and Daisy watched Hope nervously.

'You can't destroy my van,' said Grandpa.

'Why not?' asked Hope.

'Because we're both scientists,' said Grandpa. 'And we're friends.'

'We were once friends,' said Hope. 'But I can't let anything stop my plan!'

On the beach, Hope's robot moved toward the van.

Rosie didn't know what to do. But then she saw something in the sand under the van.

'Wait!' she shouted.

→ Go to page 48 for activities.

Rosie ran between the van and Hope's robot. She fell to her knees in the sand.

'Look!' She pointed down. A little brown head was coming out of the sand.

'It's a baby turtle!' she shouted excitedly. 'That means that the turtles *did* come back to lay their eggs on Turtle Island again!'

The little turtle was moving slowly across the sand in the direction of the sea.

Rosie knew that Hope could hear her. 'You can't destroy the van now!' she shouted. 'More and more turtles are going to come out of the sand here.'

Everyone watched Rosie on the big screen as she walked behind the little turtle. A hungry seagull had seen it, but Rosie waved her arms until it flew away.

'More seagulls are going to come,' said Will. 'A lot more.'

'Rosie can't keep all of them away,' said Ben.

Daisy turned to her grandfather. 'Can we go and help her?' she asked. 'Please?'

Professor Hope looked at the screen and then he looked back at his granddaughter. At last he said, 'Of course! You must go and help.'

Go to page 49 for activities.

## Chapter Eight

The two scientists watched the screen as their grandchildren helped all the little turtles to reach the sea. The seagulls above them made angry cries, but the teenagers did not let them get near the turtles.

'Look at them, Philip,' Grandpa said to his old friend. 'They're working together to help those turtles, and they're going to save them. But we can save more than just those turtles. People can care for our planet if they work together ... but you have to let them try.'

Hope's eyes were wet with tears, but he was smiling. 'You're right,' he said. He walked to his Earth Machine. The number on the clock was TWO – there were two minutes until the machine changed life for everyone on the planet.

The clock went down to ONE – one minute! – and then Professor Hope turned the machine off.

On the beach, the last of the turtles had reached the water.

'We *did* it!' said Daisy happily.

Rosie's cell phone was ringing. It was Grandpa. 'Professor Hope has switched off his machine!' he said.

Ben and Rosie were even happier when they heard this.

Go to page 50 for activities.

A few minutes later, Grandpa and Professor Hope were at the beach, too.

'I have a question,' said Grandpa. 'You use electricity on this island. How do you power all of your robots and machines?'

'I have found new, better ways to use heat from the sun to make electricity,' said Hope. 'I use energy from the wind and the sea, too.'

'You must share your ideas with everyone, Philip,' said Grandpa. 'That's how you can help the world!'

'You're right, my friend,' said Hope with a smile. 'Perhaps you can come back to Turtle Island and we'll work on my ideas together?'

Will and Daisy waved goodbye to Ben and Rosie. 'You should come, too! We're on Turtle Island every summer with our grandfather,' said Will.

It was already evening when the van arrived home.

The living room light was on but there was nobody in the room.

Ben turned off the light. 'We have to remember to save electricity,' he said. 'And we have to recycle as much as possible.' He smiled. 'If everyone does little things to help, together we can all care for our planet.'

Rosie picked up Ben's backpack. She opened it and took out her new sweater. 'And don't forget,' she said. 'We should use less plastic, too!'

→ Go to page 51 for activities.

# 🌀 **Activities** for pages 4–5

**1** **Read the sentences. Choose and write the correct words.**

**1** Rosie was in town ___buying___ a new sweater.

    **a** shopping  **b** ~~buying~~  **c** paying

**2** Ben had _____ Rosie in town for a coffee.

    **a** meeting  **b** meet  **c** met

**3** Ben put Rosie's sweater in _____ backpack.

    **a** him  **b** his  **c** he's

**4** Ben and Rosie went _____ the bus stop.

    **a** at  **b** for  **c** to

**5** Suddenly the children had a problem _____ their phones.

    **a** while  **b** with  **c** what

**6** The screens on their phones had _____ blank.

    **a** gone  **b** been  **c** taken

**2** **Circle the correct words.**

**1** People **should** / **shouldn't** use too many plastic bags.

**2** Ben didn't **want** / **wanted** to go to another store.

**3** On the bus, Rosie was listening to her **friend** / **music**.

**4** Ben was **writing** / **reading** a text message.

**5** Suddenly **everyone** / **no one** had a problem with their phones.

## Activities for pages 6–7

**1  Find and write the words.**

1  a large round object that moves
   around a star in space                    p <u>l a n e t</u>

2  to damage something so badly
   that it no longer exists                  d _ _ _ _ _ _ _

3  a form of energy that we use
   for lighting and heating        e _ _ _ _ _ _ _ _ _ _

4  basic or plain; without anything extra     s _ _ _ _ _ _

5  when something goes away and
   people can no longer see it      d _ _ _ _ _ _ _ _ _

6  the process of making air, water,
   and land dirty                   p _ _ _ _ _ _ _ _ _

**2  Circle the correct answers.**

1  What did the man say is getting worse?

   cities    electricity   (pollution)

2  What is being destroyed every year?

   the air   rainforests   animals

3  What things disappear every year?

   plants and animals    food and drink

4  What did the man have that can stop electricity?

   a battery    a machine    a car

**Talk  Do you believe the man? Talk to a friend.**

## Activities for pages 8–9

**1  Choose the correct answers.**

1  Why was the street quiet when the children ran home?

a  Everyone was too scared to move.

**b** The man's machine had stopped the cars and buses.

c  Everyone was at home watching TV.

d  Everyone was listening to the man talking.

2  Where did the man choose to test his machine?

a  across the whole world

b  in Ben and Rosie's city

c  in the rainforests of the world

d  in Grandpa's office

3  Who did the children find in Grandpa's office?

a  the man with the machine

b  Grandpa

c  a man with a robot

d  Clunk the robot

**2  Match.**

1  Ben and Rosie ran ●     ● his office, it was dark.

2  When they got to ●     ● the door of the office.

3  Clunk was at ●     ● chair was empty.

4  But Grandpa's ●     ● home to find Grandpa.

**1** **Decide if the sentences are** *correct* **(A) or** *incorrect* **(B).**

1  A few years ago, someone tried to steal
   Grandpa's work.                                      (A)  B

2  Grandpa never keeps the computer camera on.          A  B

3  The camera records everything in the room.           A  B

4  The screen showed Grandpa working.                   A  B

5  Then Grandpa wrote something on
   his computer.                                        A  B

6  Grandpa had written lots of words in
   his notebook.                                        A  B

7  Grandpa called someone on his cell phone.            A  B

8  There was a flash of light and Grandpa
   disappeared.                                         A  B

**2** **Order the words.**

1  showed / earlier. / The screen / Grandpa's office / minutes /
   twenty

   *The screen showed Grandpa's office twenty minutes earlier.*

2  in his / written / Grandpa / notebook. / had / one word

   _____

3  didn't / what / meant. / Rosie / word / know / the

   _____

**Talk** **Where did Grandpa go? Tell a friend your ideas.**

**PET**

**1** **Complete each sentence so it means the same as the first. Use no more than three words.**

1 Grandpa was in a dangerous place.

It was a dangerous place ___that Grandpa was___ in.

2 Clunk couldn't leave without Ben and Rosie.

Clunk wasn't _____ leave without Ben and Rosie.

3 The van took Clunk and the children to a beach.

Clunk and the children were _____ beach.

4 The name of the island is Turtle Island.

The island is _____ Turtle Island.

**2** **Write *yes* or *no*.**

1 When Ben and Rosie ran outside, Clunk was in the van.           ___yes___

2 Clunk wanted to take Ben and Rosie with him.           _____

3 Grandpa was in a dangerous place.           _____

4 Ben and Rosie wouldn't let Clunk leave without them.           _____

5 The van took Clunk and the children to Turtle City.           _____

6 Clunk said that Grandpa was on Turtle Island.           _____

7 There were two dark shapes coming toward them.           _____

**Talk** **What are the dark shapes? Tell a friend your ideas.**

# Activities for pages 14–15

**1 Choose the correct answers.**

1 Clunk started to move down the beach to the sea.

  **a** Right  **b** Wrong  **c** Doesn't say

2 The children followed Clunk to the trees.

  **a** Right  **b** Wrong  **c** Doesn't say

3 The two shapes on the beach were robots.

  **a** Right  **b** Wrong  **c** Doesn't say

4 Rosie felt scared when she looked at the robots.

  **a** Right  **b** Wrong  **c** Doesn't say

5 The robots looked tall and slow.

  **a** Right  **b** Wrong  **c** Doesn't say

6 The flash of bright light hurt Clunk's eyes.

  **a** Right  **b** Wrong  **c** Doesn't say

7 Clunk was moving on the ground.

  **a** Right  **b** Wrong  **c** Doesn't say

8 The robots wanted the children to leave the beach.

  **a** Right  **b** Wrong  **c** Doesn't say

9 Rosie looked at the ground, but Clunk had disappeared.

  **a** Right  **b** Wrong  **c** Doesn't say

## ⚙ **Activities** for pages 16–17

**1** **Choose and write the correct words.**

Ben and Rosie ¹ ____went____ with the robots. Then they came
to a ² _____ building in the middle ³ _____
the island. The building had a big, metal door, and there
was a camera ⁴ _____ the door. The camera moved
⁵ _____ and down – someone was studying Ben and
Rosie ⁶ _____. The children were ⁷ _____, but
then the door opened. As the door opened, Rosie saw that
⁸ _____ was waiting to meet them.

**1**  **a** did   **b** had   (**c** went)   **d** got

**2**  **a** strong   **b** kind   **c** fast   **d** large

**3**  **a** of   **b** for   **c** from   **d** off

**4**  **a** above   **b** up   **c** high   **d** top

**5**  **a** to   **b** on   **c** up   **d** at

**6**  **a** careful   **b** carefully   **c** care   **d** caring

**7**  **a** nerve   **b** nerves   **c** nervously   **d** nervous

**8**  **a** someone   **b** everyone   **c** anyone   **d** one

**Talk** **Who was waiting to meet Ben and Rosie? Tell a friend
your ideas.**

**1  Find and write the words.**

1  This is the opposite of dangerous.  s _ _ _

2  This is the color of the coats that scientists and doctors wear.  w _ _ _ _

3  This is what you do with your mouth when you are happy.  s _ _ _ _

4  This is how you feel when something happens that you weren't expecting.  s _ _ _ _ _ _ _

5  This is a university teacher or scientist.  p _ _ _ _ _ _ _ _

**2  Circle the correct words.**

1  Two **teenagers** / **robots** were waiting for Ben and Rosie.

2  Their names were Daisy and **Ben** / **Will**.

3  They had heard a **lot** / **little** about Ben and Rosie.

4  They took Ben and Rosie to a **small** / **big** room.

5  In the room there were lots of **robots** / **machines**.

6  A **thin** / **tall** man in a white coat looked at Ben and Rosie.

7  The man's name was Professor **Turtle** / **Hope**.

8  Ben and Rosie knew the man's **face** / **voice**.

**Talk** **Why did Professor Hope send the strange message? Tell a friend your ideas.**

## Activities for pages 20–21

**1** **Decide if the sentences are *correct* (A) or *incorrect* (B).**

1 Grandpa was in the big room, too.      A   B

2 Grandpa was worried that Ben and Rosie were there.      A   B

3 Professor Hope was worried about Ben and Rosie, too.      A   B

4 Now there are lots of turtles on Turtle Island.      A   B

5 Turtles used to lay their eggs on Turtle Island.      A   B

6 The pollution in the sea stopped the turtles coming.      A   B

7 The test showed Hope's machine didn't work.      A   B

8 The machine would be ready in 59 hours.      A   B

9 Rosie was very worried about Hope's machine.      A   B

**2** **Who said this? Write the names.**

1 'They'll live more simply!'      <u>Professor Hope</u>

2 'The test on your city worked well.'      _____

3 'You shouldn't have come here.'      _____

4 'But everything will be better after you use the Earth Machine.'      _____

5 'We don't have many visitors on Turtle Island!'      _____

6 'How will people live with no electricity?'      _____

# Activities for pages 22–23

**1** **Choose the correct answers.**

**1** Why did Hope give Grandpa a disappointed look?

   **a** Grandpa wanted to leave Turtle Island.

   **b** Rosie and Ben were not behaving well.

   **c** Grandpa didn't agree with Hope's plan.

   **d** Grandpa tried to break Hope's machine.

**2** How did Grandpa get to Turtle Island?

   **a** He flew there in the van.

   **b** He ran as fast as he could.

   **c** One of Hope's robots got him.

   **d** Hope used one of his machines to bring him.

**3** Why did Hope take Grandpa to Turtle Island?

   **a** He needed Grandpa to help him with the plan.

   **b** He wanted to talk to Grandpa about the plan.

   **c** He didn't want Grandpa to stop his plan.

   **d** He wanted to take Clunk from Grandpa.

**4** What were the robots going to do?

   **a** take Grandpa and the children home

   **b** lock Grandpa and the children in a room

   **c** put Grandpa and the children in the machine

   **d** give Grandpa and the children a drink and some food

# Activities for pages 24–25

**1 Order the events.**

Suddenly there was a loud noise. ____

The robots put Grandpa and the children
in a room. __1__

Something made a big hole in the wall. ____

Rosie told Grandpa what had happened to Clunk. ____

Clunk's face looked through the hole. ____

Grandpa told the children about Professor Hope. ____

They could hear Hope's robots coming. ____

Something was hitting the wall of the room. ____

**2 Look at the picture on page 24 and write *yes* or *no*.**

1 Grandpa is sitting opposite Ben and Rosie. ____

2 Grandpa is wearing a blue sweater and a green tie. ____

3 Ben is holding a photograph in his hand. ____

4 There is a photograph of Grandpa when he was
a young man. ____

5 In the photograph, Grandpa is standing next
to Philip Hope. ____

6 In the photograph, the men are standing in front of a
new building. ____

**Talk Can they stop the machine? How?
Tell a friend your ideas.**

**1** **Complete the sentences.**

> tell   look   told   ~~run~~   could   watching

**1** Grandpa told Rosie to ___run___ to the van.

**2** Rosie had to _____ the police what was happening.

**3** Hope was _____ everything on a big screen.

**4** Hope _____ his robots to get Rosie.

**5** Rosie ran to the van as fast as she _____.

**6** When she heard a sound, she didn't _____ back.

**2** **Order the words.**

**1** had / leave / Rosie / Island. / to / Turtle

_____

**2** Hope's / the room. / came / Two / robots / of / into

_____

**3** was / angry. / Professor / very / Hope

_____

**4** watched / grandfather / Will / nervously. / and Daisy / their

_____

**5** but she / tired / running. / didn't / Rosie / stop / was

_____

## Activities for pages 28–29

**1 Choose and write the correct words.**

Rosie ran. The electric fence was [1] _____ of her, but
Rosie ran through a hole [2] _____ Clunk had made.
Now she was getting [3] _____ to the van. But then
she saw [4] _____ of Hope's robots, and it was going
to [5] _____ the van first. Hope was watching
[6] _____ on his screen. He told the robot to destroy
the van, and the robot moved [7] _____ it. But then
Rosie saw something [8] _____ the van.

1   **a** on front   **b** at front   **c** in front   **d** front

2   **a** that   **b** what   **c** there   **d** how

3   **a** closing   **b** closest   **c** closer   **d** closely

4   **a** that   **b** one   **c** an   **d** the

5   **a** reaching   **b** reached   **c** reach   **d** to reach

6   **a** everything   **b** anything   **c** a thing   **d** nothing

7   **a** straight   **b** toward   **c** over   **d** forward

8   **a** out   **b** under   **c** down   **d** low

**Talk** **What did Rosie see? Tell a friend your ideas.**

**1** **Read the sentences. Choose and write the correct words.**

1 A little brown head was coming _____ the sand.

  **a** toward  **b** up  **c** out of

2 The turtles did_____ back to lay their eggs.

  **a** come  **b** came  **c** coming

3 Hope couldn't _____ the van now.

  **a** destroy  **b** disappear  **c** disappoint

4 A hungry seagull _____ the baby turtle.

  **a** was seeing  **b** had seen  **c** was seen

5 Rosie waved _____ arms at the seagull.

  **a** hers  **b** she  **c** her

**2** **Complete the sentences.**

  eat  help  coming  come  moving

1 Rosie saw a baby turtle _____ out of the sand.

2 The baby turtle was _____ toward the sea.

3 More and more turtles would _____ out of the sand.

4 A hungry seagull wanted to _____ the baby turtle.

5 Daisy wanted to go and _____ Rosie.

# Activities for pages 32–33

**1  Write *yes* or *no*.**

1  The children helped the baby turtles
   to reach the sea.                                    _____

2  The two grandfathers watched them
   on the screen.                                       _____

3  The seagulls got one or two of the turtles.          _____

4  When Hope looked at the clock, it said
   there were five minutes to go.                       _____

5  Professor Hope turned off his machine.               _____

6  Ben's cell phone rang.                               _____

7  Ben and Rosie were sad to hear that Hope
   had turned off the machine.                          _____

**2  Order the events.**

Professor Hope walked over to his Earth Machine.        ____

Professor Hope turned off his machine.                  ____

The children went to help the baby turtles.             ____

The clock on the machine went down to one
minute.                                                 ____

Grandpa talked to Rosie on her cell phone.              ____

The seagulls made angry cries above the children.       ____

Ben and Rosie were very happy.                          ____

Grandpa and Professor Hope watched the children.        ____

**1 Choose the correct answers.**

1 Grandpa and Professor Hope stayed with the machine.

   **a** Right  **b** Wrong  **c** Doesn't say

2 Hope felt sad when he turned off his machine.

   **a** Right  **b** Wrong  **c** Doesn't say

3 Hope uses energy from the sun, wind, and sea.

   **a** Right  **b** Wrong  **c** Doesn't say

4 Hope wanted Grandpa to come back to Turtle Island.

   **a** Right  **b** Wrong  **c** Doesn't say

5 Ben and Rosie didn't want to go back to Turtle Island.

   **a** Right  **b** Wrong  **c** Doesn't say

6 Will and Daisy visit Turtle Island every year.

   **a** Right  **b** Wrong  **c** Doesn't say

7 When the van arrived home, it was dark.

   **a** Right  **b** Wrong  **c** Doesn't say

8 Ben turned off the living room light to save electricity.

   **a** Right  **b** Wrong  **c** Doesn't say

**Talk Do you like this story? Talk to a friend.**

Project

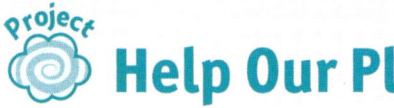

# Help Our Planet!

**1** **Do some research on different ways of reducing pollution and helping the animals and plants on Earth. Write some notes in the chart.**

**Reducing Pollution**

**Save Electricity**

______________________

______________________

______________________

______________________

**Use Less Plastic**

______________________

______________________

______________________

______________________

**Help Animals**

______________________

______________________

______________________

______________________

**Help Plants**

______________________

______________________

______________________

______________________

**Recycle**

______________________

______________________

______________________

______________________

Talk **Compare your chart with a friend's chart. Are they similar? Can you add more to your chart now?**

**2** Now read about sea turtles.

Sea turtles can be found in all the oceans on Earth except the Arctic Ocean, which is too cold. There are lots of different types of sea turtle, but they all breathe air and lay eggs. Sea turtles have a hard shell, and flippers. They swim very well, using their flippers. Sea turtles lay their eggs in the sand on beaches. When the babies come out of the eggs, they move down the beach to the ocean.

**3** Do some research on how to help sea turtles. What can people do to help protect them? Make a poster of the ways that people can help. Include some pictures. Display your poster in your classroom.

 # Glossary

**backpack** *noun*
a large bag carried on a person's back

**battery** *noun*
something that is placed inside a car engine, radio, cell phone etc. and that gives the electricity that makes the machine work

**blank** *adjective*
empty, with no pictures or words

**breathe** *verb*
to take in and let out air through your nose and mouth

**care for** *phrasal verb*
look after somebody or something

**counter** *noun*
a long flat surface over which things are sold or business is done in a store, bank, etc.

**destroy** *verb*
to damage something so badly that it no longer exists

**dirty** *adjective*
not clean

**disappear** *verb*
when something goes away so people cannot see it

**drawing** *noun*
a picture made using a pencil or pen rather than paint

**electric** *adjective*
connected with electricity; using, produced by or producing electricity

**electricity** *noun*
a form of energy, usually supplied as electric current through wires and cables for lighting, heating, etc.

**energy** *noun*
a source of power, such as fuel, used for driving machines, providing heat, etc.

**fence** *noun*
a structure usually made of wood or wire between two places, to keep people or animals in or out

**flash** *noun*
a bright light that comes and goes quickly

**heat** *noun*
heat is what makes something hot

**hole** *noun*
a space in something solid or in the surface of something

**island** *noun*
a piece of land completely surrounded by water

**joke** *noun*
something that you say or do to make people laugh, for example, a funny story that you tell

**lay** *verb*
when an animal makes an egg

**life** *noun*
the ability to breathe and grow, which people, animals, and plants have until they die

**lock** *verb*
to close something with a key

**metal** *noun*
a type of hard and shiny substance that heat and electricity can travel through

**nervous** *adjective*
worried or afraid

**planet** *noun*
a large round object in space that moves around a star, for example, the Earth

**pollution** *noun*
the processes which make air, water, land, etc. dirty

**power** *verb*
to supply a machine with the energy that makes it work

**professor** *noun*
a university teacher or scientist

**record** *verb*
to save music or video using an electronic device, so that you can listen or watch later

**recycle** *verb*
to use something again

**robotic** *adjective*
like a robot

**screen** *noun*
the flat, square part of a television, computer, or phone where you see pictures or words

**sea** *noun*
a big area of salt water; the ocean

**seagull** *noun*
a bird with long wings and white and grey or black feathers that lives near the sea

**sidewalk** *noun*
a flat part at the side of a road for people to walk on

**simple** *adjective*
basic or plain, without anything extra or unnecessary

**tablet** *noun*
a small computer that is easy to carry around with you

**tear** *noun*
a drop of liquid that comes out of your eye when you cry

**teenager** *noun*
a person who is between 13 and 19 years old

**true** *adjective*
fact, rather than a lie

**turtle** *noun*
a large reptile with a hard round shell, that lives in the sea

**visitor** *noun*
a person who comes to visit a place or to see a person

**voice** *noun*
the sounds that you make when you speak or sing

**wave** *verb*
to move your hand from side to side in the air, usually to say hello or goodbye

# Oxford Read and Imagine

**Oxford Read and Imagine** graded readers are at nine levels (Early Starter, Starter, Beginner, and Levels 1 to 6) for students from age 3 or 4 and older. They offer great stories to read and enjoy.

Activities provide Cambridge Young Learners Exams preparation. See Key below.

At Levels 1 to 6, every storybook reader links to an **Oxford Read and Discover** non-fiction reader, giving students a chance to find out more about the world around them, and an opportunity for Content and Language Integrated Learning (CLIL).

For more information about **Read and Imagine**, and for Teacher's Notes, go to www.oup.com/elt/teacher/readandimagine

**KEY**    Activity supports Cambridge Key English Test Exam preparation
 Activity supports Cambridge Preliminary English Test Exam preparation

 **Oxford Read and Discover**

How can we keep our planet clean and healthy? To find out, and to discover more about global warming and helping the planet, you can read this non-fiction book.

# OXFORD
UNIVERSITY PRESS

Great Clarendon Street, Oxford, OX2 6DP, United Kingdom

Oxford University Press is a department of the University of Oxford. It furthers the University's objective of excellence in research, scholarship, and education by publishing worldwide. Oxford is a registered trade mark of Oxford University Press in the UK and in certain other countries

ISBN: 978 0 19 473733 3

Printed in China

This book is printed on paper from certified and well-managed sources.

ACKNOWLEDGEMENTS

*Illustrations by:* Carl Pearce/Beehive Illustration.

*The publisher would like to thank the following for permission to reproduce photographs:* Shutterstock p.53 (Isabelle Kuehn).